THE LITTLE GUIDE TO
VERSACE

First published in 2025 by OH
An Imprint of HEADLINE PUBLISHING GROUP LIMITED

1

Disclaimer:

Cataloguing in Publication Data is available from the British Library

ISBN 978-1-03542-241-8

Compiled and written by: Katie Meegan
Editorial: Saneaah Muhammad
Designed and typeset in Avenir by: Stephen Cary
Project manager: Russell Porter
Production: Marion Storz
Printed and bound in China

Headline's policy is to use papers that are natural,
renewable and recyclable products and made from
wood grown in well-managed forests and other
controlled sources. The logging and manufacturing
processes are expected to conform to the
environmental regulations of the country of origin.

HEADLINE PUBLISHING GROUP LIMITED
An Hachette UK Company
Carmelite House, 50 Victoria Embankment, London EC4Y 0DZ

The authorised representative in the EEA is Hachette Ireland, 8 Castlecourt Centre,
Dublin 15, D15 XTP3, Ireland (email: info@hbgi.ie)

www.headline.co.uk   www.hachette.co.uk

THE LITTLE GUIDE TO

VERSACE

STYLE TO LIVE BY
Unofficial and Unauthorized

CONTENTS

INTRODUCTION

Versace: a family, a fashion brand, a revolution. There is no other fashion house that has shaped the landscape of celebrity and popular culture quite like the House of Versace. Steeped in opulence, glamour and a large dollop of scandal, Versace has captivated the hearts and minds of high-street shoppers and A-list celebrities alike for nearly fifty years.

The dynastic saga of Versace begins with one man: Gianni Versace. The second son of a businessman and a dressmaker, Gianni Versace took the Italian fashion world by storm in the late 1970s before expanding globally. The look that Gianni Versace pioneered is as playful as it is timeless. To think of Versace is to think of the neo-classic Medusa logo, colourful prints on quality silk, leather straps and supermodels draped in chain link gold.

A stalwart of popular culture, particularly of the 1990s, the House of Versace is synonymous with celebrity – from being the first fashion house to add musicians and actors to their front row, to being the go-to designer of Elton John, Madonna and even Princess Diana. The Versace Freedom! '90 collection of Spring/Summer 1991 is even credited with creating the supermodel phenomenon.

The success of Versace stems from the family-centred approach of the brand. From the very beginning, Gianni brought on his older brother, Santo, to run the financial end of the business and his younger sister, Donatella, as his design partner, muse and right-hand woman. It has been Donatella that has shepherded the iconic fashion house through its second act, marked by the brutal murder of Gianni Versace in 1997.

Through maintaining the classic Versace elements, as well as branching into current fashions, Versace has stayed true to the ethos of its founder; to break barriers and embrace the power of individuality.

CHAPTER
ONE

THE GIANNI YEARS

FROM HUMBLE BEGINNINGS IN SOUTHERN ITALY TO GLOBAL ICON, THE RISE OF GIANNI VERSACE IS A TALE TO BEHOLD.

FROM HIS EARLY DAYS IN THE 1970s TO THE PEAK OF HIS SUCCESS IN THE 1990s, GIANNI REVOLUTIONIZED THE INDUSTRY, AN INFLUENCE THAT CONTINUES TO SHAPE THE WORLD OF FASHION EVEN TODAY.

The story of Versace began on December 2, 1946, in Reggio Calabria, Southern Italy.

Born to Antonio, a businessman, and Franca, a seamstress, Giovanni Maria "Gianni" Versace was the second of three children.

He had an elder brother, Santo Versace, and a sister nine years his junior, Donatella Versace.

I want to be remembered [as]
a man who tried to [break] barriers
in fashion, to put fashion on the
street, to influence people in the
best way.

Gianni Versace

One of his most iconic quotes, *Little Book of Versace*, Laia Farran
Graves, 2022

My life was like a Fellini film.
I grew up surrounded by all women.
I was spoiled. I had twenty
girlfriends and twenty mothers.

Gianni Versace

On his childhood, romper.com, March 15, 2018

Gianni described his mother Franca as "ahead of her time" – she was a dressmaker who managed a workshop with over 45 seamstresses.

When Gianni was a small child he preferred learning to sew from his mother over playing outside with children his own age.

The environment was so strong, so dramatic. Tragedy is all over Calabria; it's in the air. All this corresponds to my temperament.

Gianni Versace

On the region of Southern Italy where he spent his childhood, interviewmagazine.com, June 25, 2014

When [Gianni] dressed you,
people would tell you how great
you looked and ask you where
you shopped.

Santo Versace

On his brother Gianni, romper.com, March 15, 2018

After leaving school, Gianni studied architecture in university before dropping out and returning to work with his mother as a designer and a buyer.

It was in his mother's shop where he dressed his first celebrity, Miss Italy 1970, Alda Balestra.

Gianni, he had a lot of courage. Gianni came out and said he was gay when it was very difficult to say that. 35 years ago. Even in fashion. you wouldn't say it loud. Gianni had the courage to say it loud. I'm very proud of that.

Donatella Versace

On Gianni's openness, anothermag.com, February 23, 2018

Fashion goes with the feeling of the moment. It's related to movies, to art, to young people's taste.

Gianni Versace

interviewmagazine.com, June 25, 2014

This early experience of working with a celebrity would go on to inform how Gianni melded celebrity and fashion, creating an innovative synergy that would redefine the fashion industry.

By forging close relationships with iconic figures, he understood the power of celebrity as a marketing tool and an artistic muse.

I never fall down. I always fight.

Gianni Versace

therandomvibez.com, April 1, 2023

Armani dresses the wife and Versace dresses the mistress.

Anna Wintour

The legendary *Vogue* editor on the vibe of Versace, ssense.com, 2017

In 1972, the young Gianni was hired to design knitwear in Florence but soon moved to Milan to work on his first collection under Arnaldo Girombelli, owner of the labels Genny, Compliance and Callaghan.

It's not the quality of the sketch.
It's the quality of the idea.

Gianni Versace

On his creative process, therandomvibez.com, April 1, 2023

I always claim for quality. I scream for quality, I love quality.

Gianni Versace

Little Book of Versace, Laia Farran Graves, 2022

Backed by the wealthy Girombelli family, Gianni Versace opened his own fashion house in 1978.

Originally called "Gianni Versace", he soon dropped his first name from the label, giving rise to the iconic "Versace" name.

I am not interested in the past, except as the road to the future.

Gianni Versace

therandomvibez.com, April 1, 2023

I want to be the joy to people through my work.

Gianni Versace

yahoo.com, August 20, 2018

The first Versace boutique was opened in 1978 on Milan's famous Via della Spiga.

From the very beginning, Versace was a family affair. Gianni's older brother, Santo took care of finances and after their mother's death the same year, his younger sister Donatella dropped out of the University of Florence to join him in Milan.

I had learned to love her with absolute abandon once I was an adult, when I could truly appreciate her strength.

Gianni Versace

On his mother, romper.com, March 15, 2018

Designing came to me. I didn't have to move.

Gianni Versace

luxequotes.com, February 20, 2024

Donatella and Gianni were particularly close; Gianni often dressed her and referred to her as his muse.

Donatella, for her part, often kept the "King of design" in line.

There was Santo, the calm one; Gianni, the enfant terrible, and me – Gianni's accomplice.

Donatella Versace

Reminiscing on her families dynamic, theguardian.com, September 14, 2017

Don't be into trends. Don't make fashion own you, but you decide what you are, what you want to express by the way you dress and the way to live.

Gianni Versace

harpersbazaar.com, February 3, 2022

Inspired by the Roman-Greco ruins that dotted the landscape of his childhood home, Gianni Versace adapted the symbol of Medusa, which encapsulated the spirit of Versace's powerful femininity.

Those who fall in love with the Medusa have no way back.

Gianni Versace

On the Versace symbol, ft.com, April 25, 2019

CHAPTER
TWO

A LASTING LEGACY

GIANNI VERSACE BURST ONTO THE FASHION SCENE WITH A DARING, EXPERIMENTAL STYLE THAT DEFIED CONVENTIONS, WITH VIBRANT DESIGNS, PROVOCATIVE CUTS AND INNOVATIVE USE OF MATERIALS THAT REDEFINED LUXURY FASHION IN THE LATE 70s AND 80s.

BUT JUST AS HIS EMPIRE REACHED NEW HEIGHTS, TRAGEDY STRUCK WITH GIANNI'S UNTIMELY DEATH, CUTTING SHORT THE LIFE OF ONE OF FASHION'S MOST BRILLIANT MINDS.

Elegance is the balance between proportion, emotion and surprise.

Gianni Versace

luxequotes.com, February 20, 2024

Slowly building up his reputation as a designer in Milan, Gianni Versace won the prestigious 1982 L'Occhio d'Oro (golden eye) for best designer.

This was the first collection to feature Oroton, a metal fabric made of small connecting discs with a similar texture to mesh.

Figure-hugging and shimmery, Oroton would soon become synonymous with supermodel glamour.

I think the Versace line stands between art and craft. It is not as cut and dry as one or the other but rather how they engage with each other that creates something unique.

Gianni Versace

luxequotes.com, February 20, 2024

If I did not feel I was leading from the front I would quit right away.

Gianni Versace

alainelkanninterviews.com, April 16, 2014

Gianni Versace's early style was hugely experimental, with a huge emphasis on all aspects of fabric, from how they draped to their weight and feel.

He also padded, overparred and layered textiles to create new textures and shapes.

You cannot fake chic but you can be chic and fake fur.

Gianni Versace

luxequotes.com, February 20, 2024

Even the people that say they don't care [about fashion], they care. We like to look well. In fashion, you can find beauty, quality, life. It puts colour to your life.

Gianni Versace

anothermag.com, July 15, 2022

Simplicity is the ultimate sophistication.

Gianni Versace

luxequotes.com, February 20, 2024

Luxury is anything you don't need, right? I mean, you need food, water, clothing, shelter… but chocolate, you have to survive, spiritual and emotional issues, it's all luxury, it's just how you look at it.

Gianni Versace

On the concept of luxury, luxequotes.com, February 20, 2024

Gianni Versace continuously returned to two of his favourite materials; leather and silk.

His very first solo collection in 1978 featured leather heavily. Leather was worked in different ways; blended with silk, quilted, padded, pleated and embellished forming new and surprising designs.

You have to break a barrier every day. Fashion, to me, is born and dies every day.

Gianni Versace

anothermag.com, July 15, 2022

My only dream is to get old and finally have time to read all the books that I'm collecting.

Gianni Versace

interviewmagazine.com, June 25, 2014

Silk was the second fabric pillar of Versace. Whether it was printed in bold colours, sensually draped or mixed with other textiles, silk featured in almost every Versace runway.

I think any creative activity brings risk with it. If an artist, a painter, a journalist, a director wants to do something new, he has to take risks. It's always easier to do things that already exists, things for which you have a model. Designing new things, that's difficult.

Gianni Versace

anothermag.com, July 15, 2022

"

Gianni Versace was a true
visionary and a pioneer in the
fashion industry.

"

Anna Wintour

gq-magazine.co.uk, September 25, 2018

From geometric patterns to pop art, to classical motifs and florals, animal prints and baroque designs, printed silk in bold patterns is synonymous with Versace's style.

The silkscreen printing process was labour intensive and intricate, often taking up to eight months from start to finish.

Gianni's designs often drew inspiration from classical art, architecture and mythology, creating collections that were not just clothing but wearable art.

This artistic vision laid the groundwork for future designers to explore the intersection of fashion and fine art, making it a defining characteristic of the Versace brand.

While I worked starting from a piece of art, the work itself was so inside me that the ideas were bubbling up spontaneously – I wasn't even thinking about them.

Gianni Versace

amillionsteps.velasca.com, December 4, 2017

It's copied everywhere and it's
a great compliment to give to me.
I saw this copy [in] every country,
in America, in Japan everywhere,
and I'm so pleased.

Gianni Versace

On the replicas of his S/S 1992 Tresor de la Mer print, *Little Book of Versace*, Laia Farran Graves, 2022

You dress elegant women.
You dress sophisticated women.
I dress sluts.

Gianni Versace

Never being afraid of the risqué, attitude.co.uk, April 2018

Throughout the 1980s, Versace's star continued to rise. In a strategic move proposed by his brother Santo in 1989, they launched Atelier Versace, a haute couture line, cementing their place in high fashion.

There is a Versace who is very conservative, there is a Versace who is very crazy, there is a Versace who is very theatre… I haven't decided yet which I choose to be.

Gianni Versace

anothermag.com, July 15, 2022

Fashion needs incredible women, alive, stimulating.

Gianni Versace

interviewmagazine.com, June 25, 2014

We can say that, for my brother, art was a never-ending stirring. As with his other fields of inspiration, he never copied a thing: he reinvented everything and projected it to the future.

Donatella Versace

amillionsteps.velasca.com, December 4, 2017

Women are more sure of themselves today. They don't have to emulate the way men dress.

Gianni Versace

On the fashion of women today, attitude.co.uk, April 2018

For the first Atelier Versace show in 1989, Gianni chose a luxurious silk velvet which he then painted with golden pigment, symbolizing the opulence and glamour that Versace is famous for.

Versus Versace

In 1989, Gianni gifted Donatella with a youthful diffusion line – Versus Versace, giving her a yellow diamond ring to mark the occasion.

Donatella also stepped up to the plate in 1996 to take over Versace while Gianni was recovering from ear cancer.

I design for the woman who loves being a woman.

Gianni Versace

luxequotes.com, February 20, 2024

Steeped in sexiness, glamour and excess, it wasn't long before the House of Versace courted scandal.

The Autumn/Winter 1992 collection, with its bondage and S&M themes, divided audiences and critics alike.

I don't believe in good taste.

Gianni Versace

anothermag.com, July 15, 2022

Fashion is a weapon that you can use when you need it.

Gianni Versace

luxequotes.com, February 20, 2024

Above all, my fashion has a message of freedom. I'd love to see my clothes worn by rich, by poor, by everyone. But mainly by people without taboos, because this is what poisons our life. Taboos and narrow-mindedness.

Gianni Versace

anothermag.com, July 15, 2022

I feel an artist creates things, and a designer makes things. It's a subtle distinction, but it makes a big difference.

Gianni Versace

luxequotes.com, February 20, 2024

Versace always toed the line between artistic and risqué across all his designs – including bridalwear.

The Autumn/Winter Collection 1995 made headlines as a 21-year-old Kate Moss strutted down the catwalk in a dazzling mini dress, shimmering in knee high bedazzled boots with a bouquet and veil trailing behind her.

I have a kind of repulsion for the things you are obliged to wear.

Gianni Versace

anothermag.com, July 15, 2022

Elegance is not about being noticed, it's about being remembered.

Gianni Versace

anothermag.com, July 15, 2022

I like to tell stories with my clothes. Some are sadomasochistic, some are refined, some are violent, some are sophisticated.

Gianni Versace

anothermag.com, July 15, 2022

The Autumn/Winter collection 1997, entitled the *Glory of Byzantium* was dominated by black and religious imagery.

A sharp departure from his normally colourful and opulent style, this collection would go down in history for a different reason – it would be Gianni Versace's last.

It's like I'm already living in the next century. I like to live in the future without forgetting the past. I don't know if my fashion has a philosophical or intellectual meaning, it has to do with people. Stupid or smart, chic or vulgar. What interests me is their stories.

Gianni Versace

anothermag.com, July 15, 2022

I am a lover of life, and for many years I have searched for the best way to prolong it.

Gianni Versace

luxequotes.com, February 20, 2024

On the morning of the
15th of July 1997, Gianni
Versace was returning from
a morning stroll when he
was shot twice by serial killer
Andrew Cunanan.

He later died from his
injuries in Jackson Memorial
Hospital in Miami, Florida.

He was just fifty years old.

The murder was 20 years ago.
Can't people leave Gianni alone?

Donatella Versace

Gianni Versace's murder by Andrew Cunanan has spurred
books and television. Here, Donatella expresses her frustration
at the 2018 series *The Assassination of Gianni Versace: American
Crime Story.*

ssense.com, 2018

I start work every morning [by] writing, I want to imagine women walking on the street with a simple dress – no makeup, totally different, very sophisticated – and then I translate into my designs. First thing I write down, it's like a journal every day.

Gianni Versace

On his morning routine, likely similar to the routine on the morning he was killed, anothermag.com, July 15, 2022

The funeral of Gianni Versace took place on July 22, 1997, in Milan's Duomo and was attended by the world's most famous faces including Elton John, Princess Diana and Cher.

CHAPTER
THREE

THE DOMAIN OF DONATELLA

UPON THE SUDDEN DEATH OF GIANNI VERSACE, HIS SISTER DONATELLA WAS THRUST INTO THE SPOTLIGHT AS HEAD OF THE FASHION HOUSE. JUGGLING HER GRIEF, ADDICTION AND MAMMOTH EXPECTATIONS, DONATELLA EVENTUALLY EMERGED AS A CREATIVE FORCE TO BE RECKONED WITH IN HER OWN RIGHT.

Nine years her brother's junior, Gianni Versace loved Donatella. From a young age he would dress her up and take her with him to parties until the early hours of the morning.

I was never a little girl. My brother Gianni would dress me and I would go out with a ciré jacket, a patent leather miniskirt and tall boots.

Donatella Versace

On how Gianni dressed her during her younger days, wmagazine.com, February 2, 2017

My first customer, my perfect woman.

Gianni Versace

On his sister Donatella, *Versace Catwalk: The Complete Collections*, Tim Blanks, 2021

After finishing university, Donatella moved to Milan to work with her brother.

She was his right-hand woman and vice-president of the Versace brand, often offering the female perspective to his designs.

The [couture] clothes I did in Paris are not for a grande dame de Paris. She can't wear it. I don't want her to wear it, basically.

Donatella Versace

On her clientele, anothermag.com, February 23, 2018

My style is not that big. I wear heels, tight pants and I wear diamonds.

Donatella Versace

On her signature style, wmagazine.com, May 2, 2019

To me, he was my brother, but to the rest of the world – such a genius.

Donatella Versace

On Gianni, on the 20th anniversary of his death, theguardian.com, December 5, 2017

My brother, of course, was the designer; I was working very closely with him all my life. But I started the relationship with the models that Gianni made 'super'.

Donatella Versace

On her early role in creating the "super" in supermodel, theguardian.com, December 5, 2017

For a woman to have credibility, they have to work three times more than a man… I sit on the board of directors, I'm the only woman. And I dress some of the most powerful women in the world. So, I think I'm a feminist. I show to women that you can do it.

Donatella Versace

anothermag.com, February 23, 2018

One should either be a work of art, or wear a work of art.

Gianni Versace

luxequotes.com, February 20, 2024

It was a man's society. We were not liberated; we were more conservative. But women were not sexy any more. I tried to do that, to push [Gianni] to do that. To celebrate the woman's body, and not be afraid to show real personality.

Donatella Versace

On the "blandness" and "bourgeoisie" style of the 1990s, harpersbazaar.co.uk by, March 9, 2023

It's not apologetic, it's not shy.
Unlike most of fashion.

Donatella Versace

On what makes the Versace brand so unique, anothermag.com,
February 23, 2018

Donatella was not the only member of the family involved the brand after Gianni's passing.

In Gianni's will, he had left 30% of the company to his brother Santo, 20% to Donatella and 50% to Donatella's then nine-year-old daughter Allegra.

The will was crazy, but all creatives are crazy. Gianni idolized my daughter and always called her 'my little princess,' but he put a tremendous burden on her with his will. Making headlines at the age of 11 – I wouldn't wish that on any child.

Donatella Versace

On Gianni's will, which left 50% of the company to his then 11-year-old niece, ssense.com, 2018

After we lost Gianni, I was…
destroyed, really. But I couldn't
show my pain in public because
if I crashed, then everyone around
me would crash.

Donatella Versace

interviewmagazine.com, November 28, 2011

Every life contains an event that redefines one's outlook. After that, everything is different, and the past fades. My brother's murder was that event for my children and me.

Donatella Versace

Reflecting on the momentous impact Gianni's murder had on the Versace family, ssense.com, 2018

Just over one year after the sudden and tragic death of her brother, Donatella launched her first haute couture collection.

As her brother has done before her, she built the runway over the hotel's swimming pool.

I have almost no memories of the first four months after Gianni's death. I crawled around in a tunnel of loneliness and pain.

Donatella Versace

On the grief of losing her brother Gianni so suddenly, ssense.com, 2018

"

The victory of this collection…
was that, in a state of mourning,
with so much pressure and so much
pain, Ms, Versace could produce
anything at all. She is a survivor.
And the House will be, too.

"

Amy M. Spindler

For *The New York Times*, on Donatella's first Haute Couture
collection, *Versace Catwalk: The Complete Collections*,
Tim Blanks, 2021

What is comfortable fashion?
To be comfortable, that can't be in
the vocabulary of fashion. If you
want to be comfortable, stay home
in your pyjamas.

Donatella Versace

On the rise of comfort dressing, interviewmagazine.com,
November 28, 2011

When my brother died, and the way he died, I had to show strength.
I had to show 'We're going to do it. Don't worry.'

Donatella Versace

Little Book of Versace, Laia Farran Graves, 2022

While critics were kind to Donatella's first show, it was clear that she did not find her feet until the following Spring/Summer 2000 collection, featuring bright colours and jungle prints.

One of the pieces in the collection, a green chiffon dress cut below the belly button, went on to be worn by Jennifer Lopez in one of the most iconic red carpet looks of the twenty-first century.

Gianni is irreplaceable. I would like to be judged for what I am doing, not compared to him. If you compare me to him, I can only fall short.

Donatella Versace

To a group of journalists at the opening of her first collection – Spring/Summer 1998 – after Gianni Versace's death, vanityfair.com, January 31, 2024

While others were going for sophistication and refinement, Versace tamped chic with cheekiness.

Women's Wear Daily

On the Autumn/Winter 2000 show, *Versace Catwalk: The Complete Collections*, Tim Blanks, 2021

> "People wanted more than just text. This first became apparent after the 2000 Grammy Awards, where Jennifer Lopez wore a green dress that, well, caught the world's attention. At the time, it was the most popular search query we had ever seen. But we had no surefire way of getting users exactly what they wanted: JLo wearing that dress. Google Image Search was born.

Eric Schmidt

Former Google CEO and executive chairman, gq.com,
September 20, 2019

The House of Versace is partially responsible for the creation of Google Images.

In 2000, the amount of searches for images of Jennifer Lopez's green Versace dress were so high that it caused Google to create the image search function.

As well as being Creative Director for an iconic fashion house, over the years Donatella has become an icon herself.

Not only as a designer, but for her own signature look: bleach blonde hair, waif-like figure, sky-scraper heels and dressed predominately in black.

I'm not beautiful, but I have a look: blond hair, high heels, lots of makeup.

Donatella Versace

On her image and individuality, wmagazine.com, May 2, 2019

Blonde is a way of life. You face the world like an Amazon. I survived the catastrophes in my life because of the strength that my blonde hair gives me.

Donatella Versace

ssense.com, 2018

To be blonde means to be caressed by the sun, and to be your own sun: strong, full of energy, bright, warming.

Donatella Versace

On her signature blonde hair, ssence.com, 2018

I never, ever wear flats. Every time I wear them I fall over! The only flats I own are my sneakers, which I only wear when inside the gym and always with black and diamonds.

Donatella Versace

wmagazine.com, May 2, 2019

Donatella's contributions to fashion were recognized by numerous awards.

In 2010, she won Glamour Woman of the Year, followed by the British Fashion Council's Icon Award in 2017 and the Council of Fashion Designers of America International Award in 2018.

The Versace Tribute Collection

The collection of Spring/Summer 2018 was a tribute to mark 20 years since Gianni Versace's death.

A new generation of models strutted in classic Versace designs, followed by a surprise reveal of Giannni's original supermodels: Helena Christensen, Carla Bruni, Cindy Crawford, Naomi Campbell and Claudia Schiffer.

I feel the responsibility to Gianni.

Donatella Versace

When asked how she has kept the fashion house going for over two decades, harpersbazaar.co.uk, March 9, 2023

66

[Gianni] had a love of culture and the world in general, and it would spill out into everything that he did with his designs. And obviously Donatella has that very same gene.

99

Anna Wintour

Anna Wintour on the Versace siblings, hollywoodreporter.com, October 11, 2019

I know fashion is not something that can change the world, but it can change the woman. It can empower the woman. It can make her strong, in herself, and to believe in herself more.

Donatella Versace

On the power of fashion, anothermag.com, February 23, 2018

CHAPTER
FOUR

SUPERSTARS AND SUPERMODELS

VERSACE WAS AT THE FOREFRONT
OF BRINGING HAUTE COUTURE
INTO THE MAINSTREAM BY
EMBRACING CELEBRITIES, ACTORS
AND SINGERS BOTH ON THE FRONT
ROW AND IN CAMPAIGNS.

NOT ONLY THAT, BUT VERSACE
IS CREDITED WITH CREATING
A DIFFERENT TYPE OF CELEBRITY
ALTOGETHER: THE SUPERMODEL.

No other designer understood the power of celebrity than Gianni Versace, something that Donatella Versace has carried through to the present day.

Gianni was instrumental in the emergence of the "supermodel", enlisting famous faces to strut down the runways in his designs.

He made fashion a pop culture phenomenon.

Claudia Schiffer

Model and favourite of Versace, Claudia Schiffer, anothermag.com, July 15, 2022

This was the period that fashion became famous. It was the beginning of fashion becoming pop culture, of being associated with music and rock'n'roll. Those two worlds were really in contact with one another. When something starts to happen, that is the most exciting moment. It was a huge change.

Donatella Versace

On the meeting of music and fashion in the 1990s, theguardian.com, December 5, 2017

For me, the most advanced and alienated people were often the richest, and that was worrying. I was drawn to the other side of a person, the riches and the worries in their head.

Gianni Versace

As seen on luxequotes.com by Avery Luxely, February 20, 2024

Gianni's shows were always a spectacle, blending art and fashion in the most extraordinary ways.

Cindy Crawford

Vogue, May 26, 2021

These relationships enriched both the brand and the celebrities, turning fashion into an essential component of their public personas and forever changing the landscape of the fashion industry.

In the past, people were born royal. Nowadays, royalty comes from what you do.

Gianni Versace

therandomvibez.com, April 1, 2023

The playful and confident nature of Versace attracted post-divorce Princess Diana, keen to shake off her royal image into something more sophisticated.

The icy blue silk gown from the Autumn/Winter 1991 collection is one of the most shared images of Diana in her final years.

"

I am devastated by the loss of a great and talented man.

,,

Princess Diana of Wales

On the untimely death of Gianni Versace, nzherald.co.nz, January 29, 2019

As well as styling princesses, Versace also filled the front row of his fashion shows with Hollywood royalty.

Throughout the 1980s and 1990s, illustrious guests included Madonna, Cher, Joan Collins, Uma Thurman and Demi Moore, to name just a few.

That was real a moment in the 90s when the supermodels were born, and part of what was special was that Gianni helped bring them up.

Donatella Versace

On the rise of the supermodel, interviewmagazine.com, November 28, 2011

He was the first to realize the value
of the celebrity in the front row,
and the value of the supermodel,
and put fashion on an international
media platform.

Anna Wintour

gq.com, September 20, 2019

Prince is one of the people who has been closest to me and closest to the company both in the past and now… He has always been inspiring because he is never afraid to break rules or barriers or invent something new – and if you love fashion, then you need to be able to do that.

Donatella Versace

Praising the boldness of Prince, interviewmagazine.com, November 28, 2011

I believe in luxurious taste

Gianni Versace

luxequotes.com, February 20, 2024

Gianni was a genius. He was a poet
and an artist, and he gave so much
to the world and to fashion.

Madonna

newyorktimes.com, July 17, 1997

Until Versace, there was a distinct separation between catwalk models (those who walked on runways) and editorial models (those who appeared in campaigns and high fashion magazines).

Gianni broke this unwritten rule, leading to the rise of the supermodel concept.

Fashion is all about happiness.
It's fun. It's important. But it's not
medicine

Gianni Versace

luxequotes.com, February 20, 2024

Gianni invented the supermodel concept and made these women world famous. They are rightly revered as role models because they made the leap from celebrity to globally successful businesswomen. I know few men who are as smart and enterprising as Cindy or Naomi. Their biographies can make any women's rights activist proud.

Donatella Versace

On how Gianni invented the "supermodel", ssense.com, 2018

66

It was an incredible song and an incredible designer, the moment of the women singing the song... it was like it all came together. It was like, 'OK, that's what a supermodel is.' We looked powerful – and then we started believing that.

99

Cindy Crawford

Recalling the iconic "Freedom! '90" runway walk, thesun.ie, September 6, 2023

The meeting point of music, fashion and television can be traced to Versace's Autumn/Winter 1991 collection.

George Michael cast models Linda Evangelista, Naomi Campbell, Christy Turlington and Cindy Crawford in his music video for "Freedom! '90".

The same four models closed the Versace show arm-in-arm, lip syncing George Michael's track and creating an iconic pop culture moment.

Before that, I don't think many designers let models have personality, nor after… This was totally opposite: it was about the girls, what the girls were thinking, who they were dating. It wasn't just about the clothes, but about who was wearing the clothes.

Donatella Versace

On the rise of supermodels, theguardian.com, December 5, 2017

"

[Gianni] loved for [our] personalities to shine through… [he] got us as people, humans and women rather than mannequins. Plus he was lots of fun.

"

Linda Evangelista

wwd.com, September 27, 2023

I have nothing but great memories wearing that dress and the relationship that I then went on to have with Versace.

Elizabeth Hurley

As seen on Grazia UK, "Elizabeth Hurley On THAT Versace Dress & '90s Style", YouTube, May 20, 2024.

Iconic Versace moments were and still are born on the red carpet.

In 1994, actress Liz Hurley made global headlines with a show-stopping black dress held together with golden pins bearing the Versace Medusa logo.

That, when Gianni was alive, I didn't work. That I was just around, in my high heels, blonde hair, just someone to look at. That I didn't have any specific role. I heard that so many times.

Donatella Versace

On the biggest misconceptions of her, harpersbazaar.co.uk, March 9, 2023

Real power means influencing a new generation... I want to give. Give everything I learned, gained, in the period since Gianni was no more.

Donatella Versace

On how losing Gianni changed her outlook on life, wmagazine.com, February 2, 2017

I would like to be a rock star, if I had talent. But I don't.

Donatella Versace

On what she would be if she wasn't a designer. As seen on wmagazine.com by Steph Eckhart, May 2, 2019.

The first time I wore it, I actually didn't have another dress. Usually I have choices. It was a last-minute thing that caused a sensation that was unexpected.

Jennifer Lopez

On the sensational green dress that became iconic, glamour.com, January 14, 2020

He made women look strong and glamorous. He had this amazing ability to create something that was both powerful and beautiful.

Cher

As seen on vogue.com by Sarah Mower, August 1997.

Music and musicians have always been an important part of the Versace universe.

Elton John and Prince have both performed custom music for Versace shows.

More recently, Dua Lipa co-designed a Versace collection in 2022 and Bruno Mars released a sultry hit with "Versace on the Floor" in 2016.

I dress the noveaux riches. So what?

Gianni Versace

On the snobbery of the fashion elite, *Fashion Gamebook: A World History of 21st Century Fashion*, Florence Muller, 2008

Liam Gallagher was in the audience. He got up and started to walk with the models and I was like, 'Sit down!'

Donatella Versace

Reminiscing about her 1995 men's show, where Robbie Williams and Tupac performed, gq-magazine.co.uk, September 25, 2018

66

I remember for my first Versace
show, everyone was very surprised
because no one really saw me as
the runway type. But you believed
in me from the moment we met.
You always said it's not about
changing yourself to be on the
runway. Be yourself and honour
your body.

99

Gigi Hadid

Thanking Donatella Versace for helping get on to the catwalk,
interviewmagazine.com, February 23, 2018

I find it incredible when I go to rock concerts. I went to one recently and all these young people were screaming, 'Donatella! Donatella!' I was like, 'Let's leave.'

Donatella Versace

On becoming famous herself, gq-magazine.co.uk, September 25, 2018

Fashion and music are the same, because music expresses its period too.

Gianni Versace

Drawing direct parallels between the worlds of fashion and music, luxequotes.com, February 20, 2024

With Versace still dressing today's hottest celebrities, there is no end to the amount of show-stopping looks that have been provided by the fashion house for some time now.

CHAPTER
FIVE

BEYOND THE RUNWAY

VERSACE HAS NEVER BEEN CONTENT TO REMAIN WITHIN THE BOUNDS OF TRADITIONAL WOMENSWEAR. UNDER VISIONARY LEADERSHIP, THE BRAND EXPANDED INTO MENSWEAR.

BUT THE VERSACE EMPIRE DIDN'T STOP THERE – FRAGRANCES, ACCESSORIES AND DIFFUSION LINES FOLLOWED, ALONG WITH LUXURIOUS HOME COLLECTIONS AND EVEN A LINE OF PALAZZO VERSACE HOTELS, EACH EMBODYING THE LUXURIOUS, EDGY SPIRIT OF THE BRAND.

Comfort is very important to me. I think people live better in big houses and in big clothes.

Gianni Versace

yahoo.com, May 13, 2021

It is often difficult for people to perceive that a designer can be so deeply involved in the creation of every single detail, and I am so deeply involved.

Gianni Versace

Answering the question of whether he signs off on every Versace detail, luxequotes.com, February 20, 2024

Many men would like to wear this, but they are afraid – afraid to dress, afraid to be ridiculous, afraid of their friends who wonder why they aren't putting on a jacket and tie... In an age like ours, things should be more free and democratic.

Gianni Versace

On the restrictions of men's fashion, anothermag.com, July 15, 2022

He liked sexy men. And men like to be sexy. And not only gay men. I realize that heterosexual men like to be sexy more than gay men, honestly!

Donatella Versace

On how Gianni Versace would approach menswear, independent.co.uk, January 12, 2014

Diffusion Lines

Versace's diffusion lines are
sub-brands that offer accessible luxury,
blending youthful designs with the iconic
aesthetics of Versace.

Versus Versace

Versace Jeans Couture

Versace Sport

Versace Home

Young Versace

Versace Collection

I think glamour all the time. I wake up in the morning and I'm already thinking glamour.

Donatella Versace

Vogue, September 23, 2016

Fashion is frivolous, and many people keep it at arm's distance and are slightly ashamed of it. But it's full of glamour and open to all.

Gianni Versace

luxequotes.com, February 20, 2024

I was very determined that men today are liberated. With all this oppression going on in the world, through your clothes you can be who you are, or who you want to be in the moment… Well, through my clothes.

Donatella Versace

On modern masculinity, independent.co.uk, January 12, 2014

Versace's impact on menswear was often seen in the wardrobe of *Miami Vice* – the show became a world of brightly coloured shirts eye-catching prints.

Silk printed shirts (in a variety of prints and colour palettes) have featured in nearly every Versace menswear collection.

Some would say that it was Versace that introduced true colour into men's wardrobes.

I never forget the Medusa, the Greek, the sexuality. Because sexuality is very important, men's and women's, in the collections. Not a vulgar sexuality, but sexuality is a big part of each of us.

Donatella Versace

On the Autumn/Winter 2015 Menswear Collection, gq-magazine.co.uk, October 6, 2015

The suit does so much for a man.
I love how a man looks when he is
wearing a suit.

Gianni Versace

luxequotes.com, February 20, 2024

Gianni Versace's love of leather also found its way into menswear collections.

This rock'n'roll style was quickly adapted by contemporary musicians such as Elton John, Bono, Prince, Jon Bon Jovi, Lenny Kravitz and Zayn Malik (who co-designed a capsule collection for Versus in 2017).

I want to create the basic wardrobe of a man – not necessarily a different man, but a better dresser.

Gianni Versace

luxequotes.com, February 20, 2024

I am surrounded by impossibly sexy men. Sorry! That's my reality! How can you think about not making them sexy?

Donatella Versace

independent.co.uk, January 12, 2014

I think it's the responsibility of a designer to try to break rules and barriers.

Gianni Versace

therandomvibez.com, April 1, 2023

Ever the innovators, Versace has embraced co-ed fashion shows featuring both womenswear and menswear on the same runaway, such as the Spring/Summer 2021 collection, demonstrating that fashion is not limited by gender norms.

If I was to design a failure of a collection tomorrow, it wouldn't worry me in the slightest. I don't pay much attention to the critics.

Gianni Versace

anothermag.com, July 15, 2022

No fashion house would be complete without a fine of perfumes and Versace is no exception.

The first Pour Femme eau de toilette, *Gianni Versace*, was produced in 1981, followed by *Versace L'Homme* launched in 1984.

Be yourself. Trust your instinct.
My brother always told me that.

Donatella Versace

On the wisdom of Gianni Versace, interviewmagazine.com,
February 23, 2018

There are numerous scents for Versace and its diffusion lines: Eros, Crystal Noir, Versus, Dylan Blue and Yellow Diamond.

In 2019, Donatella Versace launched six new upscale unisex perfumes under the Versace Atelier.

Perfume puts the finishing touch to elegance – a detail that subtly underscores the look, an invisible extra that completes a man and a woman's personality. Without it there is something missing.

Gianni Versace

therandomvibez.com, April 1, 2023

I think to be superficial, you have to be very profound.

Gianni Versace

anothermag.com, July 15, 2022

Versace Home

The commitment to living Versace extends into the home.

Introduced in 1982, the Versace Home collection features luxurious items, from bathrobes to light fixtures, infused with bold colours and the iconic Medusa motif, creating a lavish lifestyle.

I can't sit in a super-modern chair.
I like the rich.

Donatella Versace

independent.co.uk, January 12, 2014

My house reflects a great love for classicism and a strong attraction to certain old English mansion that transmit a sense of safeness. It is full of collections I am fond of, and to me it is a home in a very deep sense.

Gianni Versace

On his Miami home, architecturaldigest.com, June 14, 2023

Even Michelangelo got paid for doing the Sistine Chapel. To those artists who say they're doing it for the love of art, I say: 'Get real'.

Gianni Versace

therandomvibez.com, April 1, 2023

Palazzo Versace

In 2000, The first Palazzo Versace hotel was created in Australia, located on the Gold Coast.

First developed under the direction of Gianni before his tragic death, the concept was expanded and further developed by his sister, Donatella.

The second location opened in 2016 in Dubai, while the third opened in 2020 in Macau. The hotel concept continues to embody Versace's opulence, showcasing the designer's iconic style and attention to detail.

I know that Palazzo Versace will continue this warm welcome for every guest who comes to visit, for many years to come.

Donatella Versace

macaonews.org, March 25, 2024

If you're not blind, you can find
fashion everywhere.

Gianni Versace

anothermag.com, July 15, 2022

The impact of the House of Versace on fashion and culture cannot be denied.

Mired in scandal, opulence and celebrity, the Versace family will continue to intrigue us for decades to come.

Some say Versace is a genius, others say Versace has no talent. But I believe neither the one nor the other, I believe in working every day, I believe in excitement in everything that makes me happy as a man and as a working person.

Gianni Versace

anothermag.com, July 15, 2022

I think that is the ultimate luxury, to feel good about yourself and to make the most of what you have.

Gianni Versace

luxequotes.com, February 20, 2024

"

I live as I please.

"

Gianni Versace

alainelkanninterviews.com, April 16, 2014